Capture your market.

An Introduction to Marketing Management

Kevin Griffiths MSc

DEDICATION

Without any doubt I would have never completed this paper without the support and encouragement of my wife Franciska. A big thank you to you and our children Rebecca, Lucas, Victoria, Cassandra, Olivia, Noah and Isabella for giving me the time, space , understanding and love needed to complete this task. Your sacrifice does not go unappreciated.

Thanks also to The University of Liverpool and Laureate Education who provided the motivation and resources for me to complete this work during my studies for a MSc in International Management.

ACKNOWLEDGMENTS

Thanks also to The University of Liverpool and Laureate Education   who provided the motivation and resources for me to complete this work during my studies for a MSc in International Management.

Marketing Management

As consumers become more aware and sophisticated, the process of marketing needs to evolve and advance in its mechanisms. Broddy (2008) states that " All organisations face the challenge of understanding what customers want, and ensuring they can meet those expectations."The simple concept that the process of marketing is all about strategic placement of advertisements to meet organisational objectives has developed into a more sophisticated mechanism for delivering messages in a more complex way. Thematically the shift in delivery systems means that the critical focus should remain. That is, the organisation goals will remain the same, better sales, greater awareness or some other message, the strategies employed must take into account the increase in consumer awareness. These changes in audience understanding are the driving factors of being able to get the message across. No matter which contemporary approach or view we take to marketing the outcome of the delivery mechanisms remains the same.

With globalization the need to communicate quickly and effectively is more paramount. In the high tech markets the need to establish product first is one of the key drivers. With large budgets and a large experienced marketing team the major players had in the past, the advantage as pointed out by Meldrum (1995) "A further problem, especially for small business, is that large organizations, and/or ones which wield power in an industry, are usually able to exert considerable influence in the setting of standards by having people qualified and available to sit on a standards body, by being able to insist on their inclusion and by being in a better position to influence market perceptions" As a result of competing with the major players campaigns for the small emerging companies there was a need to develop new fast traveling low cost ways of communicating messages. This resulted in the pro-active use of the internet. On-line marketing ,social networks and viral campaigns have played a critical part in launching new products to a global market. Ramirez (n.d) points out that "Online social networking and social media marketing are an amazingly cost effect means of spreading the brand message and building both customer rapport and loyalty." These new methods of marketing have been so successful that large international organisations are now employing these techniques.

We can see the shift in delivery methods of messages within the "not for profit" sector. Over the past few years we have seen charitable organisations adopt and adapt marketing strategies to increase awareness of issues and enhance fund raising activities. This has been a difficult process but one that has paid off. Two areas that are contentious are direct mail and legacy campaigns. It was only because of the success of these new ways that the professionalisation of "not for profit" sector marketing and promotion activities is becoming more acceptable. The emergence of relationship marketing plays a new and valuable role in promoting and developing the aims and objective of many "not for profit" organisations. During the mid nineties I worked for the fund raising dept. of the British Red Cross. At this time the organisation was undergoing radical change and there was a major cultural change within the marketing and fund raising depts. One of the key marketing objectives was to communicate to the membership the need to employ more commercially based marketing practices for the benefit of the organisation.

Understanding and accepting that customers are more aware and in tune with marketing techniques is a theme that purveys through the development of marketing strategies in today's globalization of markets.

Conceptual framework of market orientation.

Marketing trends and strategies designed to capture audience participation in an organisations goals that focus on the conceptual framework of 5 emerging principles identified by Lafferty and Hult (1999). Based on market orientation the principles allow for a framework that permits the development of strategies that meet the goals of the organisation while working on the premiss that customer values and wants drive the organisational goals. By focusing on the customer it has become vital for organisation staff to "buy in" and have ownership of the identified values and the mechanisms employed to implement the strategy. By embedding the principles of market orientation throughout the organisation the staff are able to remain on board and on message. we shall look at the emerging principles and assess the described frameworks and the applications within current organisational activities.

Hyper-competition is driving rapid an revolutionary changes in the way organisation innovate and capture competitive advantage. By covering the needs of the customer and counter-balancing the activities of competitors the organisation can enhance and develop the distribution of its message and brand. Reviewing Lafferty and Hult (1999) perspective of the following market orientated activities, (1) the decision-making perspective; (2) the market intelligence perspective; (3) the culturally based behavioral perspective; (4) the strategic perspective; and (5) the customer perspective, we can begin to account for there impact and effectiveness within today's markets.

The decision-making perspective.

In line with the general trend of organisational structure, the policy of cross organisational communication is a fundamental. By instilling and exploring customer and market trends and needs from distant and internal information sources the collective can calculate and react to market needs in an innovative fashion.

The market intelligence perspective.

Information gathering is the key to developing effective and clear messages. One of the skills maximized within this perspective would be the ability to identify future trends. As Kohli and Jaworski (1990) cited by Lafferty and Hult (1999) identify the assimilation of information from many integrated and independent sources are required. This information should be delivered and responded to in a inter-organisational manner.

The culturally based behavioral perspective.

Understanding the customer in an global market is a multi tasked approach. Accepting and incorporating mechanisms that account for and adapt to differences in cultural perspectives, understanding and activity are key processes of activating successful campaigns. The same could be said of an organisations competitors as well as identifying weak areas that can be targeted for competitive advantage. The information gleamed from identifying activities must be distributed and acted upon on an organisational wide basis.

The strategic perspective.

The use of information and the empowerment of managers to collect and act on information in a strategic sense is a critical part of an organisations ability to develop and satisfy consumer need. By identifying needs of customers we can manipulate strategies around organisational goals to accommodate the customers perceived need and deliver on internally driven aims.

The customer perspective.

Focusing on the customer in a singular manner is a cultural approach that may be best suited in areas that demand high customer value and internal or external market domination in niche markets. Otherwise solely focusing on the customer may critically damage internal innovation and growth potential through lack of competition knowledge and positioning.

As Lafferty and Hult (1999) identify "Three of the five models indicate the need for the organization to generate and utilize information on competitors as well." This indicates that there is a growing understanding for the needs of the customer through the delivery mechanisms and strategies of the competitor. The customer and competitor are intrinsically joined as defined by Sørensen (2008) "Customer orientation and competitor orientation are each defined symmetrically to market orientation, incorporating the components of generation and dissemination of intelligence and action." This trend of interdependence within organisational structure is symptomatic of the changes within organisational structure in a hyper-competitive environment, more free flowing information and innovative means of implementing strategies that are formed by the dissemination of information have become a cultural part of all departments within organisations.

When we look at the effects on the profitability of market orientation through customer value, transference of information and the strategic delivery of corporate and sales messages we can see that it plays an important part in reaching a level of understanding with the customer. The impact of market orientation within companies was highlighted by Lancaster (2004) "results in business performance make it worthwhile to implement market orientation programmes." In conclusion we can see that the future of organisations will rely on its understanding the direction and needs of its existing and future customers, market orientation is a key driver in meeting these needs.

Decision Making

The process of embarking on a family visit to a restaurant requires both collective and individual decision processes. For a decision to be made there needs to be at least two options available for a decision to be made. We will explore the activities undertaken to decide a venue and the information available and its use in attaining a consensus. There will also be decisions made on an individual bases that may or may not impact on other individuals within the group. Kacem & Lee (2002) "The tendency to focus on group preferences and group harmony in collectivist cultures leads to an ability to repress internal (personal) attributes in certain settings. Accordingly, people in collectivist cultures often shift their behavior de-pending on the context or what is "right" for the situation". Factors that impact on an activity of this nature would involve identifying an environment that is conducive to the majority of the group. How we attribute or perceive an establishment, the activities used by the venue to attract customers and how that meets the needs of the group/consumer, influence the final decision.

The fundamental activities of establishments in reaching and persuading potential customers to frequent their venue will play a significant part in the groups decision making. Each member may attribute that information in a way that meets their own individual views and perspectives. The attraction of a fast food outlet may attract children with free gifts with food, the parents may see this as unhealthy food but would be willing to patronize the establishment to please the children against their better judgement . One could say that the comments of Linn (2004) "Given the intensity and pervasiveness of marketing to children, it is either cynical or naive to assume that individual parents should bear the sole burden of shielding children from the potentially harmful effects of a $15 billion industry." are an escape for parents in a high pressure consumerist approach to food. Decision making against sophisticated marketing will require objective criteria establishment, something that can be difficult so alternatives can be presented that may deflect from the influences of the larger food chains.

In conclusion we can see that the influences on families when going for a nice family visit to a restaurant release a wide range of commercial influences, free gifts, low prices and established character figures. While we may attribute a specific culture to the organisation we can also be impacted by the type of food available. This is becoming more important as we identify with "healthy choices" so much so that the issue is being addressed by fast food chains and used to influence parents as a method of counter pointing established view points. As a parent I wish to provide my children with healthy food in a fun environment, while I have doubts about the fast food chains I can see that they have identified this general concern and are addressing it in the promotion of their product. Marketing through education is proving a strong influence, this dissemination of information is identified by Mizeski et al (1979) "An information source could affect the stability of consumer's attribution through the consistency dimension by providing education or instruction." Identifying the spin and the education of food marketing is a difficult process that requires expert understanding and evaluation, a resource not available to most consumers.

A Date with Data

We meet with data collectors on a daily basis and the general view is that its a part of a modern day life or at least something that we should accept. However, there appears to be an increase in consumer awareness in connection with data collection and growing concerns of invasions of privacy and risk of identity theft. One of the driving factors of this awareness today is in the emergence of identity theft, in particular when it concerns finance. Looking at two particular arrears of data collection and action monitoring, loyalty cards and on-line shopping, we will examine changing approaches by the consumer. While

Graeff,& Harmon (2002) addressed a growing concern about the use of personal data and monitoring of individuals purchasing actions, even though concerns were highlighted, there was a degree of acceptance by the consumer. This growing awareness may not change purchasing habits with established organisations but will make consumers more sensitive to providing data to unknown bodies.

Graeff,& Harmon (2002) said that "Just because a consumer is concerned about how their personal information is collected and used does not mean that he or she will reduce their amount of purchasing." However since 2002 there has been increased awareness around data collection, at one of the UKs leading retailers and operator of a loyalty card scheme,Tesco, Humby (2004) identified that "One of the consistent problems with loyalty programmes is that while customers are enthusiastic about participation in the process, when confronted with the volume of data that the company running the scheme has collected, they are less comfortable." Loyalty cards still play a major part in the Tesco marketing strategy and will continue to do so as long as the public are willing to continue to 'sell' information to them. Issues around privacy do not come into play because the individual is not forced to participate in the 'selling' of their information.

With increases in on-line shopping since 2002 we can see that consumers are more willing to give information about themselves and their financial information. This may be due to the efforts of banks and organisations, like PayPal, that have established secure methods of collecting information. Even with this increase in confidence or willingness to participate in transactions on-line Listerman & Romesberg (2009) highlight that "the rate of data breach incidents has risen more than 400% since 2005" in connection with on-line identity theft.

When we look at the issues around gender and demographics in parting with information there seems to be a variance in who is more concerned. Graeff,& Harmon (2002) indicated that males were less concerned about privacy issues and how the information maybe used although higher income individuals were more likely to want to now what the information would be used for. Although Park (2008) found that "Gender did not play a significant role for the respondents' beliefs in on-line privacy rights" As the consumer becomes more aware of the issues and hazards of providing information then any demographic differences in attitude will dilute, as seen with the time difference, six years, of two papers quoted here.

The practice of collecting, selling and using of data collected from consumers will continue to play an ever increasing role in the marketing activities of organisations. There will be a need to reassure consumers that the information they provide will be safe and only used for agreed purposes. The data protection laws enacted in the UK and other countries go some way to protecting the individual from legitimate traders in data. A higher awareness of how and when the individual delivers data will play a major role in determining the collection processes of the future, already we can see on-line activity that encourages individuals to 'sell' personal information for points, samples or even cash rewards. Our date with data will flourish into a long term relationship that will impact on all aspects of our lives.

Product Development

Producing a limited range of product that

satisfies consumer need and establishes brand identity is an effective way of sustaining an organisations market development. The ability to identify specific customer groups is key to product development and introduction. This segmentation can be affected by both geographic and socio-economic variables and organisations should modify marketing activity to account for this. However, we should recognise that the development of production systems means that there can be variations in final product format. This variation can give the perception of a wide range of products but is in fact just a process of construction of added value packaging.

Although the approach of a few general products targeted at 'Mr average consumer' could be seen as a safe way to capture market share, we must be aware of the faster moving and changing attitudes to product development by consumers. In particular in the technology sector, which as a hungry consumer base, needs to segment its market in numerous ways to continue to sell. While the basics of computer hardware remain the same,the targeting of niche markets within the segmented audience is a critical part of successful sales. The segmentation of the PC market has moved to mass customization with Dell among others allowing consumers to design and customize the PC they feel they need. This, Kara & Kaynak (1996) 'finer segmentation' could be seen as the way forward. With technological and production advances the concept of mass customization is going to play a larger part of global organisation strategies. Kara & Kaynak (1997) "the number, variety and assortment of products manufactured will be substantially higher than that available under traditional segmentation"

Organizations face the dilemma of focusing on mass customization or limiting potential growth by focusing on more traditional segmentation, even niche areas could become vulnerable if attention is not paid to a growing desire by the consumer for more personalization of products and services. There will be a growing move towards creating mass customization in areas that have traditionally focused on either mass production or output focused on broad area of segmentation, either cultural, geographic or socio-economic. The future is for the individual. Although Fogliatto & Silveira (2008) state that

"At the operational level, process flexibility capabilities should correspond to those products and features being most valued by customers." we will see marketing activities in a wide range of markets directing consumers to a perceived individualization of product, creating a uniqueness to ownership. This means that as Kotler &Keller (2009) identify "..the key is adjusting the marketing program to recognize customer differences"

We can see that segmentation plays an important part in the profitably of an organisation, but that segmentation needs to evolve into mass customization as the more discerning consumer opens up to more flexible and specific product needs. How organisation strategically embark on this will be to some extent be determined by their industry and the consumer profile and as Kara & Kaynak (1997) say "it is generally recognized that there is no one best way to segment markets, as each approach has certain merits and limitations". As their is no best way then the opportunity for innovation is very prominent and vital for the expansion and enhancement of the consumer sector. The future of profitability is in the identification of, and the desire generation in the individual customer to have a product made for them. This mass customization is an extension of Henry Fords objective of supplying "one for all". With the new technology in production and delivery systems the 'one for all' is still a very potent sales pitch, only today it means a unique product not a mass produced one.

Lifestyle and the travelers dream: The future of tourism.

Looking at the development of the tourist industry over recent years and how trends determine choices and how changes in lifestyle and economic prosperity influence consumer choice is a crucial mechanism in developing new and innovative holiday choices. The influence of lifestyles and the simplifying of travel opportunities has given the tourist industry a strong growth, even in times of economic difficulty the trend towards rest and relaxation is still high on the individuals agenda. The influences that determine choices of destination and activity are linked to the aspirations of the consumer. To meet the needs of these consumers marketeers are embarking on greater segmentation to facilitate the demands of a consumer who is more aware, better educated and less afraid of new destinations than the early days of package travel.

To better understand the full potential of market share, organisations are moving towards greater segmentation of it customer base. This segmentation as been noted on a basic level for most tourism stakeholders by Tkacynski et al (2008) that "Most tourism stakeholders profile their tourists using between two and four segmentation bases. The most common variables used to profile tourists were activities sought (behavioral), location (geographic), income (demographic), trip purpose and motivations (psychographic)." However, in light of greater choice for the consumer this over simplified approach may be derogatory to the aims of the tour operator. The upturn in self arranged holidays means that tour operators need to source more exotic or special interest holidays out of reach of the average tourist. This requires greater understanding of drivers in lifestyle and 'dream-style' environments of the potential customer. In their research Gonzalez & Bello (2002) segmented the market "into five clusters: home-loving, idealistic, independent, hedonistic and conservative." The needs of the customer may well be based on a hierarchy of travel motives as highlighted by Gonzalez & Bello (2002). These motivators are becoming more sophisticated and demanding no matter which area of segmentation we look at. In the past holidays were an opportunity to withdrawn from everyday life. Now holidays are about enhancing our lifestyles. This as resulted in a more diverse and complicated approach to capturing market share. Tkacynski et al (2008) "Today's tourism marketers must influence consumer decision making in an increasingly complex and competitive global marketplace."

There are now many factors that determine the choice of the consumer that fall outside the normal destination- activity sphere. Pan et al (2009) "Tourism is a combination of many sectors that, in turn, influence and are influenced by other sectors." The external influences today include fears of terrorism and pandemic, these fears must be addressed by marketeers and governments to ensure the sustainability of the industry. The consumers desire to use the holiday as an extension of their lifestyle is highlighted by Pan et al (2009) "Travel has become more activity-interest based" The focus on lifestyle segmentation by marketeers will out of necessity become more integrated in the lifestyle of consumers.

Gonzalez & Bello (2002) have laid the path for understanding the choices being made by a knowledge rich audience. Alternative approaches to tourism should now be seen as the normal approach. The growing sophistication and finer segmentation of market audiences will ensure that customized holidays remain high on the agenda of tour operators. The success will be in identifying efficiently the segmentation trends and communicating availability without moving away from the consumers lifestyle.

Is PLC PC?

The role of marketing within and in relation to the product life-cycle (PLC) is a symbiotic relationship covering all stages, Introduction, Growth, Maturity and Decline. Each area requires a specific action or actions from the marketing team. It will be important that the marketing team monitor and evaluate the activity of the product within its different stages of the cycle. Being able to process the flow of the product will enable the seamless introduction of new product at the end of the cycle. Understanding this cycle and its role is a crucial element for product development and advancement. There is an issue with whether PLC is a reliable measure of the life of a product and that it could be a way of dictating the demise of a product.

It is important to be able to place the product at a particular point at any given time to allow for future planning and development. This could be a difficult task as highlighted by Dhalla Yuspeh (1976) as cited by Grantham (1997) "..it is possible to assume a product is at a particular phase when the opposite may in fact be the case." Miss placing a product within the cycle could have a negative impact in terms of future product introduction, profitability and brand awareness. There is also a risk that the product could be undervalued within its market because of the drive to introduce new product. This need to rapidly develop may lead to organisation shortening the life-cycle of a product in favour of a newer shiner successor. Placing too much focus on a theoretical process runs the risk of the product not having its full potential fully realized even if re-branding or re packaging may be required towards the end of the process. The marketing team should play a significant role to ensure that potential of a product is achieved and deter their organisation from over introducing new product while there is still life and profit in the existing model, whether re-packaged or re-branded. There is also a risk that the natural positioning of the product could be missed by theoretical marketing strategies and programmes. Creativity and innovation should be employed to introduce and sustain a product. Marketeers should look at the whole picture and not focus on pre-designed delivery mechanisms, there will be times when the PLC model will fit the product, but it should be viewed as a strategy option only.

With certain products the life cycle is not the 'product' but its target audience. Products that are targeted toward specific evolving targets like an age based groups then the PLC takes on a different momentum requiring the management of all for stages at once as the consumer migrates through the stages associated with this reverse PLC. The product may require re-packaging to ensure it is relevant to current thinking and trends. This scenario is high-lighted by Broody (2008) with the case of Lynx deodorant which targets 15 - 24 year males and therefore needs to introduce and recruit a new customer base of 15 -19 year olds. This type of market means that the product can reach maturity and avoid or significantly delay the onset of decline.

Marketing should not be seen as a reaction to PLC but as an intrinsic part of the entire life-cycle, however, because there is the chance that by following a PLC path it will result in a self fulfilling road to being discontinued. Kotler & Keller (2009) "the PLC pattern is the self-fulfilling result of marketing strategies and that skillful marketing can in fact lead to continued growth." Marketing teams must have a broader view of the market and the consumer.

Brand Space - Getting the bigger picture.

With globalization and the development of rapid information transmission systems the role of the brand manager is becoming a more complex. Understanding the position of the brand and its impact on the consumer will allow greater opportunity for brand sustainability. Taking the brand identity and communicating messages around that brand at different phases of it customer relationship requires the brand manager to identify with the needs of the consumer and the organisation.

Understanding the complexities of a brands status and functionality in the market within the framework of "abstraction and enactment" as defined by Berthon et al (2003) allows for more analytical approach to future development and sustainability of the brand. Identification of this 'Brand Space' outlined by Berthon et al (2003) as four quadrants defined by two axes that allows the brand manager the mechanism for placing and managing a brands development. This framework defines the current position of a brand and will allow for a more targeted approach to keeping the brand on message through consumer understanding. The methods of evaluating a brands position and the issues of reassigning a brand image were faced by Berthon et al (2003) who recognized that "many firms have faltered badly in their attempts to extend their brands by moving them into different product categories," Failure to keep the identity or associations of a brand will lead to the potential failure of its linked products as Berthon et al (2003) point out "perceptions of a brand arise from information they receive about it from the company, other customers and third parties"

The application of the Brand Space framework is a useful mechanism for reviewing and managing the complexity of brand positioning and new product vs new brand introduction in global, multi-cultural environment. An organisations lack of understanding of its brand, and the equity in that brand, as on occasions led to new product ranges not naturally associated with the original branded product to fail, while product extension is likely to be more successful Ambler & Styles (1996) cited Sullivan (1992) "…the probability of a brand extension surviving more than six years could be as high as 93 per cent when the extension is launched into a mature market, as opposed to 75 per cent for new brands…" the development of new product ranges is not as likely to capture the heart of the consumer unless the brand as a high abstraction value. We can see the development of the Virgin brand as being able to cross consumer barriers from a Cola to Space Travel. Although the issue of Virgins brand could be questioned in regard to its equity because of the personality association with Richard Branson, the equity may well be in Branson. Brand identity is a sensitive matter and can be damaged by miss association or through association with negative historical actions, e.g. Exxon, and the pollution of the Alaskan coastline and Nestle and the baby formula issue. Nestles programme of providing free formula milk to mothers in developing countries resulted in a worldwide boycott of their products. What was perceived as a positive action in fact became a negative because of the perception that Nestle were exploiting mothers in poverty. Personality association with brand management and development is a risky bond and requires careful management. Entire organisations can be damaged if the associated individual is exposed for some wrong doing e.g. Martha Stewart.. As brands are linked to non product activity through sponsorship of events as a way of linking brand with an ideal or value they run the risk of exposing the brand to negative association. Association with sport for example could adversely effect a brand if that sport or an individual are identified as cheating or using drugs. Failure to maintain emotional and historical value in a brand is becoming a greater risk for brand managers as the information and mis-information world plays a growing role in dissemination of opinion.

Not understanding where the brand fits in the 'brand space quadrant' could seriously impact on the the market development and consumer perception. Critical assessment of non brand space issues should also be accounted for when implementing brand awareness, growth and development. Brand managers must understand the personality of the brand and how it interacts with the consumer. Errors of not connecting brand with the emotional ties of the consumer can lead to a movement away from the brand or as in the "New Coke" case a consumer rebellion and product U-turn as highlighted by Berthon et al (2003). Managers should recognise that brand development is an evolutionary process and will need to assign its development in incremental stages taking into account the attachment by the consumer to the historical context of the brand. We can conclude that the 'brand space' framework can play a role in placing and communicating brand image and message, but only when there is full understanding of the total organisational and consumer environment.

Picking the Price

Price should be seen as a way of communicating with the customer. The factors involved in establishing that price are the determiners for success. A consumer should identify a perceived value to trigger a purchasing action. For the price to be right the marketing manager should evaluate a range of factors both internally and externally to the organisation. There seems to be a trend in not reviewing in depth the issues around pricing. The majority of organisations seem to focus on a 'cost plus' system modified to market trends. While the control of price can be determined by effective management of production and material costs, the service industries need to assess more closely the activity costs associated with the service delivery. Specialist technology based products need careful strategic processes to enable effective, valued placing in the market. Novelty and technological advancement can play a major role in assigning a need value and premium price allocation.

A critical mistake that can be made by organisations is to avoid looking at other strategic issues when setting a price. By focusing on a policy of cost plus decisions a company can miss opportunity to maximise on profit and market development. Avlonitis &

Indounas, (2005) "a clear implication for managers responsible for pricing decisions within their firms is to move away from these simplistic cost-plus formulas and treat pricing from a customer's point of view in all the steps of their pricing process."

When reviewing the pricing structure for a new innovative technological product a strategy of developing a 'must have' profile will help to maximise price and recoup high R&D outlay.

Using a high entry price can be risky but it is a strategy employed by many high technological companies including Sony as identified by Kotler & Keller (2009). Apart from the costs associated with the Research and Development of the product there will be issues around the production costs and volume attribution. Once the factors around development and production are accounted then issues around customer value perception come into play. The development of a product profile linked to the Brand is a key element of internal price development influences. Zeithaml (1988) " price is but one of several potentially useful extrinsic cues; brand name or package may be equally or more important "

This can be seen with Apples introduction of the iPhone. "Apple's pricing strategies include setting the price high at the start of launching a new product" Sliwinska et Al (2008). The internal driver to reclaim the expenditure associated with the R&D plays a significant part in Apples introduction pricing policy. However, in terms of prestige the high introduction price increases the perceived value and need of the product, buy also limiting availability of the iPhone Apple added to the 'must have' effect. Apple have avoided the 'cost plus' approach in determining the setting of the introductory price of the iPhone by linking price to the internal strategic and brand marketing policies of the organisation. 'Cost Plus' pricing and going rate pricing strategies will come into play as competitors introduce new products that compete with the trend setting product. This can be seen with the introduction of the second generation iPhone 3G.

When introducing new ground breaking technology it is important to position the products price by taking into account factors such as generating high value and need in the eyes of the customer. This will allow for the development of a larger market at later stages of production or introduction of a Mk2 product. The price of a product has the power to communicate many messages including uniqueness, value, brand identity and desirability. Reviewing all the internal corporate drivers like brand image, marketing strategy, corporate profile, production/distribution and R&D will all contribute to setting the right price.

Delivering the goods

How organisations get their products to the customer in a global market requires the organisation to assess the ways in which it facilitates the delivery of the product to the final consumer. Where timing and availability are key to the distribution of a product, the producing company must measure the resources available internally, and the external impactors, for smooth delivery to the final destination. Successful resource efficient delivery in a fast moving market is a step toward competitive advantage. It is because of changing environment that the view of, and practicalities of, distribution systems are evolving to accommodate global and localised supply chain networks.

For organisations to ensure they produce and deliver products to the consumer in the most efficient and profitable manner they need to remain in control of the entire supply chain. Conventional methods of distribution through independent agents means there is a greater risk of breaks in the supply chain. As each member of the chain is driven by their own goals and objectives there could be the opportunity for conflict of interest and lack of motivation to meet the needs of the producer and the consumer. By taking control of all parts the the supply chain an organisation can more realistically control the output of those parts. However, one could argue that because there are different skill requirements within the various elements of the chain the diversification from producer to wholesaler, distributor and retailer could dilute the operational efficiency of the organisation. Also it maybe that, as identified by Wuyts et al (2004) that "buyers value a sequence of strong ties that run from suppliers through the vendor to the buyer " This can only increase the motivation of organisations to acquire the skill sets needed to gain greater control over the supply chain.

The need to compete competitively and profitably means that organisations need to look at all the mechanisms employed to deliver product to the consumer. By making the channel to the customer more transparent and controllable organisations are taking on more diverse activities and actions to achieve competitive advantage. Satellite television broadcaster Sky recently acquired the independent developer/manufacturer of their set top box, Amstrad. This acquisition meant that Sky would have total control of the development and output of the production process, more enabling them to meet the growing needs of the market. Speaking to the BBC chief executive James Murdoch(2007) said."It will help us to drive innovation and efficiency for the benefit of our customers," Sky also added that "the deal would "significantly" reduce costs in its supply chain"

The movement into controllable delivery systems is going to be a critical element in most organisations development in the future. Whether this movement from the conventional marketing channels to one of the Vertical Marketing Systems (VMS) is through Corporate VMS, Administered VMS or

Contractual VMS it does mean that organisations will require more influence and control of the supply chain, dependent on their resource availability. Frazier (1999) "As the world economy evolves, more and more companies are highlighting channel management as among their very top priorities"

Advertising Problems

Entering new geographic markets for a US pharmaceutical company can pose many issues, in particular how to communicate the benefits of a product or brand of specific drugs to the consumer and dispenser. The many issues including cultural attitudes, consumer influence and legal restrictions will mean that the marketing strategy would need to be adapted from that of the companies home market. Within the The United States there is a driving movement to promote specific drugs directly to the consumer, with the under lying, or in some cases not so underlying message to get the consumer to ask their doctor to prescribe a specific branded drug. There are within the US three activities of communication for pharmaceutical companies.

1.   Direct   to   Consumer Advertising:

incorporating multi media distribution of information specifically targeted to public mass audiences, including TV, Radio and Print.

2. Detailing: This is the direct one to one or seminar approach of disseminating information and directing doctors to prescribe specific brands of drugs to their patients or drug purchasing departments of hospitals.

3.Other Marketing Efforts: The use of specialist Print and other technology based delivery methods targeted at professionals within the prescribing sector.

To enter the European market it will a requirement to adjust campaigns to meet legal requirements and restrictions. While in the US DTC is used to promote prescription drugs it is not currently permitted within Europe, although non prescription drugs may be advertised to the consumer. It become necessary to refocus efforts within Europe. There is an EU commission proposal Article 88a of Directive 2004/27/EC to allow the dissemination of information to the consumer via the internet as pointed out by Parmar (2009).

With restrictions on DTC for their prescription

drugs companies would need to focus on the "detailing "element of encouraging doctors to prescribe and hospital drug purchasers to stock their drugs.

There would also be an increase needed in trade and professional print advertising to help offset the lack of consumer knowledge regarding drug availability.

To implement drug education with the consumer is a more complex matter outside of the USA and may be better for the consumer in relation to the need and perceived need for specific treatment.

This lack of consumer knowledge may be a positive in respect of a prescriber because they are not put under pressure to prescribe inappropriate drugs. Although the view from the industry is different Parmar (2005) argues that "DTCA provides a favorable environment for shared decision-making wherein the patient is aware of the risks and benefits of new drugs". Berndt E.R (2005) highlights the issue of persuasion "Many of these advertisements do more than simply inform consumers about the availability of a drug; they also attempt to persuade consumers to use it"

No matter the view or interpretation of the issues the company must operate within the law and that means where DTCA is prohibited the focus of promotion must fall to Detailing in the main, supported with other marketing efforts within the trade and professional media.

Detailing and OME are the accepted methods within the more regulated markets of Europe and Asia and they must become the driving arrears for a US pharmaceutical company's inroad into their new marketing areas.

With DTCA has a growing possibility of introduction within Europe and Asia, Taylor and Raymond (2000)"With the continued economic liberalization of Taiwan, PRC, and Korea and the strength of the Japanese market, many more changes in the advertising industry are expected." and while there is potential for greater consumer awareness, the argument for DTCA from the industry, it is important from a consumer perspective to be aware that heath issues are diverse, complicated and driven by the individuals non medical knowledge.

Implementing Marketing

Success for an organisation is dependent on

its ability to communicate a broad range of messages to its customers, suppliers and staff. The art of marketing over the last 30 years has seen a tremendous change in mindset and delivery mechanisms. While traditional approaches have been focused on sales objectives, today we see a more holistic approach . The need to convey specific messages externally and internally to assist in the achievement of organisational goals require marketing teams to implement, monitor and react to campaigns. In a global market the position of competitive advantage is in most cases vulnerable to challenges and hence requires adaptive and responsive actions through marketing channels. Failure to act out the delivery systems of a marketing plan and then monitor and accommodate necessary changes will lead to positional and market loss. Modern marketing is a multi-disciplinary act operated through diversified delivery systems.

Theoretical approaches to marketing and the development of marketing plans may look good in the boardroom but if the motivation to implement, deliver and pro-actively monitor the plan is lacking then it is set up to fail. The motivation of organisations to take on marketing activities on an inter-departmental level requires that systems of efficient communication are established as identified by Ryals & Knox (2001) change in working practices so that information is shared between departments to build up a picture of the firm's total relationship with the customer. Effective actioning of a marketing plan will need to be monitored and adapted through time. This monitoring is dependent on Motivation, Opportunity and Ability to process measurement data as identified by Clark et al (2005). The desire by an organisation to follow through its plan should be a major priority. Having established within the organisation the status of the plan it should then establish mechanisms to react to incoming data. This will help ensure functional success of the marketing plan.

Flexibility and responsive marketing plans in a fast moving and expanding environment become the key to successful fulfillment of marketing objectives. Plans that are comprehensive and regimented and fixed do not allow for adaptation within fluctuating markets. Slotegraaf and Dickson(2004)" marketing plans that are comprehensive may inherently produce rigidity effects".

This rigidity is going to result in unresponsive and non adaptive actions that could lead to market loss or lack of understanding of internal and external messages.

How organisations succeed in their marketing highlights how poor implementation will lead to reduced output, lower sales and poor brand recognition. Maintaining control of an integrated marketing plan is one of the keys to global success. Manchester United football club is a good example of how controlling the marketing strategy and internal implementation of the marketing plan can lead to one of the strongest global sporting brands. This strategy of total control based on the success of the team and the individual personalities linked to the club results in MU being a major brand around the world. Broody (2008) states that "The management believes this enhances the ability to deliver branded services to customers any where in the world" Failure to identify and react to the marketing plan would result in poorer recognition and branded sales.

Functional application of a responsive holistic marketing plan is a critical part of an organisations fundamental make up. The marketing plan is not a paper exercise but a fully functioning organic process within a cross departmental system of multi channel communications.

ABOUT THE AUTHOR

Kevin Griffiths has over 30 years experience in developing new and emerging organisations in both the commercial and the 'not for profit' sector. He lives in Ireland and travels extensively. He has also published **Management of Eco-tourism and its Perception: A Case Study of Belize**

Contact: kevin@jaffamedia.com

www.ingramcontent.com/pod-product-compliance
Lightning Source LLC
Chambersburg PA
CBHW061519180526
45171CB00001B/254